VICTORIAN
PUBLIC HOUSES

Crown Liquor Saloon, Queen Victoria Street, Belfast

VICTORIAN PUBLIC HOUSES

Brian Spiller

David & Charles : Newton Abbot

TO MILLICENT

ISBN 0 7153 5697 6

Set in 10 on 12pt Bodoni
by C E Dawkins (Typesetters) Limited London SE1
and printed in Great Britain
by Latimer Trend & Co Ltd Kent
for David & Charles (Publishers) Limited
South Devon House Newton Abbot Devon

CONTENTS

PRIVATE HOUSE TO PUBLIC HOUSE

Until the nineteenth century, inns and public houses looked like private houses, except for the sign indicating that refreshment was available. With the spread of literacy, the painted or three-dimensional figures of white harts and red lions, black horses and green men, were replaced by the name of the house, displayed in bold lettering across the façade. The advent of a new commercial era, in which beer was no longer brewed on the premises but supplied by a public brewery, was marked by the appearance of the company's advertising board, as at the Bell & Anchor, Hammersmith, above. Faulkner's history of the parish, 1839, from which the picture is reproduced, notes that this tavern adjoined the first turnpike on the Great West Road, and that 'the magistrates have ever found it convenient for business, the rooms being appropriately fitted up and appro-

priately arranged. The present proprietor has made great improvements and additions'. Unfortunately for him, the trunk roads were about to lose their traffic to the railways. Hammersmith, still largely rural in 1839, doubled its population by 1866, by which time the customers of the Bell & Anchor were mainly Irish labourers from the neighbouring slums.

The point of this case history is that the trade of public houses is peculiarly sensitive to environmental disturbance and to shifts of population. And the aim of this book is to illustrate some of the ways in which the English public house responded to economic and social pressures, to changes in the law and to the rise in the standard of living, in the seventy years between the Great Reform Bill and the death of Queen Victoria.

7

London's population rose from under a million in 1801 to over two million in 1841, offering great rewards to the manufacturers who could distribute their products most efficiently, and to the retailers most skilled in displaying them. The movement to improve shopfronts, using the novel combination of plate-glass and gas-lighting, was compared by Dickens to an epidemic disease that had worked its way through drapers and haberdashers, chemists and hosiers,

> when it burst forth with tenfold violence among the publicans and keepers of 'wine-vaults'. From that moment it has spread among them with unprecedented rapidity, exhibiting a concatenation of all the previous symptoms; and onward it has rushed to every part of town, knocking down all the old public-houses, and depositing splendid mansions, stone balustrades, rosewood fittings, immense lamps, and illuminated clocks, at the corner of every street.

The architect J. B. Papworth, according to his son and biographer, designed 'the earliest of the gin-palaces', Thompson & Fearon's, 94 Holborn Hill, in 1829-31. It figures in the rhyming caption to Cruikshank's caricature, above: 'the bell chimes to church and out stagger the queer 'uns, from Wellers in Old Street and Thompson & Fearons'. Edward Gibbon Wakefield singled it out for mention in 1833: 'Here gin is served by young women dressed up like the *belle limonadière* of a Paris coffee house, and the establishment in all its parts is nearly as fine as *Verey's* or the *Café de Paris*'. A hundred others could be seen within half an hour's walk:

> Every one remarks the increase of gin-shops. In all those parts of Leeds or Manchester, and of London too, where the poorest people live, there you find, in almost every dirty street, not one but several fine houses, handsomely stuccoed, curiously painted, ornamented with plate-glass and polished brass . . . [and] inside, great

barrels of spirits gaily painted and disposed for show, carved mahogany and more polished brass, with men and women, smartly dressed, smiling welcome to all who enter.

The gin-palaces of the 1830s were built and fitted out on a far more lavish scale than the gin-shops of the previous decade, not just because there had been a general retail revolution, but as a result of political manoeuvres. Almost every significant change in the drink industry can be traced to an act of Parliament. In the 1820s, the public was agitated by fears that gin sales were rising, and beer sales falling, because gin cost too little and beer too much.

'Free trade in ale and alehouses' was the grand panacea tried out in 1830, when Wellington's government abolished the beer duty and brought in an act permitting any ratepayer to sell beer for 'on' or 'off' consumption in his own dwelling-house, without a justices' licence. The paymaster-general, introducing the bill, said it was designed to give 'the poor and working classes . . . a chance of obtaining a better, cheaper and more whole-some beverage'. This object would be achieved by 'throwing open the trade'. Expectation was rewarded; 24,000 new beer-houses had opened by the end of 1830, and 46,000 by 1836. The price of 'fourpenny' beer fell to 2d per quart pot, and 'twopenny' sold for 1d. The sale of spirits also fell, although it regained the old level by 1838 and by 1845 was much higher. That was not the end of the story. The gin distillers, like the brewers, belonged to a capital-intensive industry that was quite capable of defending a threat to its market. They too, at this period, financed publicans in return for their custom. Gin-palaces, in densely inhabited areas, were a powerful counter-attraction to beer-houses. In turn, hard-selling methods and their social consequences stimulated the growth of the temperance party, which began as an anti-spirits movement. The cartoon, above, is from George Cruikshank's *Sketchbook*, 1835.

9

George Cruikshank

The new beer-houses, and many of the old ones, offered the simplest amenities. One in Scotland Yard, Westminster, was described by Dickens in *Sketches by Boz* and illustrated by Cruikshank, above. Every object in the room is for use. Its regular customers, coalheavers in working clothes, drink Barclay's porter in pewter tankards. The dog on the hearth symbolises the quasi-domestic character of the scene. Opposite: the kitchen of a country beer-house, drawn by 'Phiz' and

10

engraved by Ebenezer Landells for the *Illuminated Magazine*, January 1845. Here the dog is a poacher's lurcher and the centre of attention a radical agitator denouncing the game laws. This little drama illustrates one of the reasons why the new beer-houses were not regarded by all land-owners as an unqualified success. Palmerston, writing as home secretary in 1853, described them to Gladstone as 'Haunts of Thieves and Schools for Prostitutes. They demoralise the lower classes . . . The words "licensed to be drunk on the Premises" are by the Common People interpreted as applicable to the Customers as well as to the Liquor'. The other point of interest in this picture is that it shows what went on before there was a bar. A corner of the kitchen has been partitioned off, left, and secured with a heavy lock, to form a beer-store or 'tap-room'. This partition, which might be pierced with a hatch or consist merely of a rail, was the rural equivalent of the bar counter and served the same purpose: to prevent the customers from helping themselves and from getting in the way of the servers. When in the course of time the kitchens of such public houses reverted to private occupation, 'tap-room' (or its shortened form 'tap') became the generic name of the ordinary public room. Genteeler customers would be shown to the 'parlour'.

'Tap-room' and 'parlour' are the names given to the public rooms in J. C. Loudon's *Cyclopaedia of Cottage, Farm and Village Architecture*, 1833, which devotes fifty-two pages to designs and descriptions of country inns and public houses.

The bar is defined by Loudon as 'the office, to which all enquiries are addressed, and from which all orders are issued', with the qualification that 'in small public houses and inns it is used as a shop or store-room, as well as an office'. The only

1316

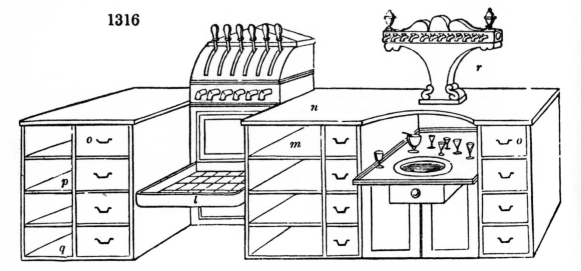

12

example of this combination of use is a design for a suburban public house, where the 'shop' is described as an area where customers drink standing at the counter or bring their own jugs and bottles to be filled. Two drawings illustrate Loudon's point that 'the fitting up of public house bars in London forms almost a distinct trade'. Opposite, above, is a 'view . . . looking towards the bar from the shop, and supposing the counter to be removed'. Here the bar is a store-room and serving space, accommodating 'store vats for such liquors as are sold in larger quantities, and these are drawn directly from the vats by cocks'; smaller casks connected by pipes to the counter; 'bins for wines and liqueurs kept in bottles' and 'pigeon-holes for bottles containing choice compounds, cordials, etc.' with shelves for glasses and 'pewter or stone pots for beer, ale, etc.' Opposite, below, is 'a view of the inside of the counter, looking from the bar-room'. The 'fountain', right, has cocks for dispensing liquor

piped from the small casks. It is flanked by a 'six-motion beer-machine to draw the beer and ale of different ages and qualities from butts in the cellar'. The need to meet heavy demand was the reason why a semi-mechanical means of dispense had become necessary in large urban public houses a generation or two before country beer houses were equipped with a counter. By 1810, for example, the Crown, Fleet Street, had 'a Three Motion Beer Machine with Pewter Sink, Lead Pipe, Screw Cocks and apparatus complete, fix'd in a neat Mahogany Case'. In the next stage of the bar's evolution, the bar back-fitting was devised to bring bottles, glasses, tankards and the taps of barrels within arm's reach of the servers. In terms of technical equipment, the contemporary rural tap-room, page 11, is still in the Stone Age, and it may be inferred from the photograph of an urban public bar of 1896, page 82, that there had been no innovation in the intervening half-century.

13

The magnetic power of the gin-palace to attract the urban proletariat was the theme of many caricatures by George Cruikshank. He is a hostile witness. His father had 'died of drink' and he himself 'signed the pledge' in 1848. On page 13 is a plate from *The Drunkard's Children*, published in the same year. The caption runs: 'Neglected by their parents, educated only in the streets, and falling into the hands of wretches who live upon the vices of others, they are led to the gin-shop, to drink at that fountain which nourishes every species of crime'. An earlier volume, *The Bottle*,

had described how the family was ruined as the result of the father, a respectable young man, drinking a glass of gin. Dickens, reviewing *The Drunkard's Children*, was moved to complain that this sort of propaganda was misleading:

Drunkenness, as a national horror, is the effect of many causes. Foul smells, disgusting habitations, bad workshops and workshop customs, want of light, air and water, the absence of all easy means of decency and health, are commonest among its common, everyday physical causes. The mental weariness and languor so induced, the want of wholesome relaxation, the craving for *some* stimulus and excitement, which is as much a part of such lives as the sun is; and, last and inclusive of all the rest, ignorance, and the need there is amongst the English people of reasonable, rational training, in lieu of mere parrot-education, or none at all, are its most obvious moral causes.

Cruikshank, unabashed, continued as before, delighting temperance meetings, when he was over eighty, by dancing a hornpipe on the platform as proof of the healthy effects of abstinence. Opposite: a plate from his *Temperance Peepshow*, issued by the Band of Hope in the 1850s. Below: a drawing by William McConnell, reproduced from George Augustus Sala's *Twice Round the Clock in London*, 1859. It represents a 'gin and beer palace' opposite the Royal Victoria Theatre (The Old Vic) at the half-time interval. Sala identifies the customers as 'honest, hard-working mechanics, their wives and families', sailors, a lifeguardsman and an 'Ethiopian serenader'. They are obviously enjoying themselves. McConnell conveys a mood of pleasurable animation in a scene where Cruikshank chose to record misery, degradation and vice.

CLASS DISTINCTIONS

Alphonse Esquiros, a French writer and socialist politician who lived in England in the 1850s, believed that the public house supplied much evidence about the structure of English society. First, there was the 'bar-room', where all sorts of London types congregated: organ-grinders, Punch and Judy showmen, sellers of hot eels or watercress, Jewish dealers in old clothes. 'The bar-room is the antechamber to the public house': here one was served at the counter, drank standing up, or passed on:

> The other divisions of the public house are the tap-room and the parlour. The tap is the meeting-place of mechanics and artisans . . . The parlour, cleaner, better lighted, better decorated, in a word, more 'respectable' as the English say, is generally frequented by persons of the lower middle class, tradesmen, clerks, actors, obscure literary men and reporters. It is furnished with tables, isolated to some extent from one another by wooden screens of a certain height, against which they are set. Separation in unity—there is the whole of English life . . . The tap has no communication with the parlour, for the entire economy of English society depends upon a strict separation of the classes.

The company varied from district to district, from house to house and from bar to bar. Esquiros explains that 'some of these establishments are very large, with pretensions to sumptuous good taste. The bar is attended by pretty girls, well dressed and reserved in manner', and 'presided over by a stately publican, assisted by pot-boys . . . Here, all is quiet enjoyment, light and comfort, combined with luxury'. Other extremes were represented by the village alehouse with white-washed walls and sanded floors, where country-men discussed racing and the state of the crops,

and the smoke-filled dens in the slums where 'the poorer classes seek bitter consolation for the habitual evils of an uncertain life'. Churchwarden or Broseley clay pipes were commonly sold or hired out by publicans. A tobacco box was displayed, from which a fill could be had by inserting a halfpenny or a penny.

Opposite: a drawing by John Tenniel, from *The Gordian Knot*, a novel by Shirley Brooks, 1860, delineates the tap-room of 'a small public house in a squalid street inhabited chiefly by sellers of birds and stealers of dogs'. Local residents used these houses as clubs where they could escape from their homes and families. This is a self-contained, male-dominated community; everybody hopes that the child dancer and her mum will soon go away. There is no attempt to decorate. Matchboarded walls and ceilings, hard furniture and sanded floors are perfectly suited to the customers' mood. They drink, not the gin advertised on the walls, but porter in pewter pots.

'Until comparatively recent years', Charles Booth wrote at the turn of the century, 'the publican's customers were very particular as to their ale being served in "a nice bright pot", and the essential virtue in a potman was that he should be a good pewter cleaner; the pot is however now being largely supplanted by the glass'. Connoisseurs of draught beer believed that it tasted better in the traditional material, an opinion endorsed by Calverley in his advice to undergraduates:

He that would shine, and petrify his tutor,
  Should drink draught Allsopp in its 'native
                                         pewter'.

Above: the scene in the parlour of a market-town inn where the hero of George Meredith's *Evan Harrington* is subjected to the scrutiny of local farmers and commercial men. Glasses of wine and spirits are on the table. The illustration, by Charles Keene, is taken from *Once a Week*, where the novel was serialised in 1860.

Public houses in the new housing estates on the fringe of early Victorian London manifested the outward and visible signs of inward respectability demanded by their clientele. The Drapers Arms, Barnsbury Street, Islington, above, stucco classical, dates from about 1843. The Royal Hotel, Norland Road, Shepherds Bush, opposite, built about 1851, later changed its name (sometimes an indication of unsatisfactory trading) to the Havelock Arms, reverting to the original title between 1876 and 1881, when this photograph was taken. It was quite common for public houses to appropriate the designation 'hotel'. Some were large enough to accommodate guests for bed and breakfast, such as the Albion, Epsom, which advertised a charge of 2s 6d (12½p). The choice of the name 'Royal Hotel' may also have owed something to the licensed trade's aspiration to higher social status at a time when the prohibitionist party was making sustained efforts to bring it into disrepute.

The anti-spirits movement of 1829-30 had been institutionalised with the formation of the British and Foreign Temperance Society, interdenominational but run by Anglican clergymen, financed by rich philanthropists and pledged to moral persuasion and moderate reforms. This platform was unacceptable to working-class radicals and nonconformists such as Joseph Livesey, who believed that moderate drinking of wine or beer was morally wrong, and that anything short of total suppression of the 'liquor traffic' must be an ignoble palliative. The passion, energy and ruthless tactics of the militants enabled them to win a mass following for 'total abstinence' at the cost of alienating upper-class and moderate middle-class opinion. Queen Victoria, patron of the Church of England Temperance Society, was well **aware of the distinction between** temperance and 'teetotalism' when she wrote to her prime minister:

Osborne, 10th Feb. 1894

The Queen has approved Canon Basil Wilberforce's appointment, but wishes to add a condition to it, viz., that he should not, when preaching at Westminster, use the very strong total abstinence language which he has carried to such an extreme hitherto. Total abstinence is an impossibility; and, though it may be necessary in individual cases, it will not do to insist on it as a general practice; and the Queen relies on Mr. Gladstone's speaking strongly to him in this sense.

19

Opposite: the Warwick Castle, Warwick Place, Maida Vale, built in the mid-1850s, when its discreet location in a cul-de-sac may have made it a refuge for domestic servants from the neighbouring stucco villas and terraces. Well over a century later, it still draws some of its custom from these massive houses, long since servantless and often divided into small flats. The intimacy of the Warwick Castle's small scale and its atmosphere of an earlier period, derived from its old-fashioned fittings, appeal to the nostalgia of the middle class. Mews public houses in Belgravia have undergone a similar change of use.

Above: the Pakenham, Knightsbridge Green,

photographed between 1875 and 1882, declares its purpose in handsome raised Egyptian lettering above the second storey. One's eye is led upwards to the sign, not the Pakenham family's coat of arms, as one might expect, but a delicate representation of two racehorses in low relief. This must have been added after Tattersall's auction rooms moved to the same street, not much more than a whip's length away, in 1864. The number of blocked windows suggests that the building pre-dates the abolition of the window tax in 1851. Vine leaves, bunches of grapes and bearded faces of bacchants are the motifs of the frieze above the windows of the second floor.

The Café Central, White Lion Street, Norwich, was a public house located in the heart of the city's business quarter. Its best room, above, and its public bar, opposite, were photographed about 1900. Hard chairs and multiple pulls for serving draught beer are the characteristics common to public bars. There is no sign of a beer engine on the counter of the superior room, where the shelves are stacked with wines, liqueurs, spirits and cordials. The rest of the room is furnished like the sitting-room of a private house, with an oil painting in a gilded frame, an ornamental clock on the mantelshelf, a rug before the open fire, and button-down seating ranged against the walls. Even here, of course, the furniture is designed for heavy wear, notably the cast-iron 'Britannia tables'. The two pictures illustrate the general point made about this time by Charles Booth:

It is the aim of the publican to give to each compartment some convenience or attraction

of its own, be it publicity or privacy, a snug corner or a 'jolly crush-in'. It is his object to separate the classes for whose wants he caters, and he can do it by the style in which the drink is served as well as by its quality and by the price charged in different bars. These arrangements, adjusted locally to the character of the particular districts, seem entirely to suit the peculiarities of the English social class system. The people sort themselves and, whether from above or from below, regard with friendly indulgence, devoid of envy or contempt, the habits and weaknesses of others.

According to the *Westminster Gazette* in 1899, it was customary for a public house to have 'three open rooms, freely inviting class distinction—the saloon, the parlour and the tap-room'. However, the names of the public rooms and their significance have differed from one period to another, and vary today according to the locality and the

status of the house. There is a broad difference in usage north and south of the Trent. 'Bar', unqualified, or 'public bar', means the room where furnishings are simplest and prices lowest. The latter term is generally, though not exclusively, used throughout the country. 'Tap-room', an older name, is its equivalent, mainly in the North, together with 'vaults' and its variant in Lancashire, 'vault'. The better furnished of the two basic public rooms is called 'saloon bar' in the South and 'smoke-room' in the Midlands and the North, excluding the North-East, where it is the 'sitting-room'. There may be a third, best-furnished room, generally called the 'lounge', with 'parlour' as a synonym in the North. The 'private bar' was used to accommodate groups who wished to keep to themselves, including men accom-panied by women or, in the absence of a 'ladies' bar', women only. Some bars were imitations of foreign models. The 'buffet', where one ate standing at a counter, took its name from the refreshment rooms of French railway stations; and the origin of the 'American bar' and its modern equivalent, the 'cocktail bar', is evident in the words used by Dickens, describing an hotel in Boston, Massachusetts:

There is no smoking-room in any hotel, and consequently there was none in ours; but the bar is a large room with a stone floor, and there people stand and smoke, and lounge about, all the evening; dropping in and out as the humour takes them. There too the stranger is initiated into the mysteries of Gin-sling, Cocktail, Sangaree, Mint Julep, Sherry Cobbler, Timber Doodle, and other rare drinks.

NEW TASTES IN DRINK

The brewers' signboards tell a story of changing tastes in beer. 'Entire', an abbreviation of 'entire butt beer' (so called because it was originally brewed in imitation of a popular mixture drawn by publicans from casks of different beers) had been the staple drink of heavy manual workers since the eighteenth century. 'Porter' was the colloquial name for this dark, heavy-bodied, bitter-tasting beer; and 'stout' a stronger, more expensive version. The pale, lighter-bodied ale preferred by the upper classes began to penetrate the mass market after 1845, when repeal of the excise duties on glass encouraged the bottling of beer for the home trade and the substitution of

glass for pewter tankards. These innovations favoured 'drinking by the eye' and therefore the bright, sparkling product against its dark competitor. The main beneficiaries were the brewers of Burton-on-Trent. They had learned, not only how to imitate the leading export brand, Hodgson's India pale ale, but how to make a better product, because the Burton water, very hard and highly charged with gypsum, had exactly the properties required for the production of pale ale. That is the answer to the second part of the Shropshire Lad's rhetorical question: 'Say, for what were hop-yards meant, or why was Burton built on Trent?' A generation before Housman, a pale ale from Middlesex, a Dublin stout and two pale ales from Burton were apostrophised, not too seriously, by C.S. Calverley:

O Beer! O Hodgson, Guinness, Allsopp, Bass! Names that should be on every infant's
tongue!

Shall days and months and years and
centuries pass,
And still your merits be unrecked, unsung?
That omission was repaired when advertising to the masses really got going. In the meantime, brewers ensured that their names, if not lisped in every nursery, were presented to every spectator's eye. So the Talbot, 75 Borough High Street, Southwark, opposite, one of the last of London's coaching inns, demolished in 1875-6, served as an advertising site for Allsopp's pale ale on the spot where Chaucer's pilgrims started their journey to Canterbury. The name of Southwark's local brew, Barclay Perkins' porter, is set out on the lower signboard. It was common for publicans to advertise, and for London brewers to make, both types of beer: above, the Spaniards, Spaniards Road, Hampstead, photographed in a time when it was possible to stand on the road and stare without meeting a violent death.

25

Above: the Red Cow, 11 Prince's Street, Lambeth, photographed between 1866 and 1869, the years when the Albert Embankment was being built, in the course of which this rough neighbourhood—note the powerful figure of the publican, left—disappeared. The other figures in front of this archetypal building are the bearded potman, wearing the emblem of his trade, the apron needed to protect his clothing when drawing beer from the wood; a customer in a dustman's or coalheaver's hat and moleskin trousers, and a potboy, employed to fetch and clean used tankards. On the signboards, lettering of marvellous elegance and panache whets the demand for Whitbread's porter, double stout and pale ale. By 1843, there were only three brewers in London—Reid, Meux and Courage—who did not brew pale ale, and the great porter houses were being challenged by the ascendancy in many

London coffee-houses and taverns of Guinness's Dublin stout, 'a respectable enough drink', despite contemporary allegations of 'sub-acidity and soda-water briskness when compared with the balmy character of London bottled stout from a crack brewery'. As it turned out, Guinness made the more accurate estimate of the future trend in taste, although the London brewers of stout successfully defended their share of the market into the next century. Opposite above: Reid's stout, Courage's porter, with Allsopp and Courage ales, are advertised at the Bell & Hare, 724 High Road, Tottenham, then a free house, along with 'billiards', 'luncheons', 'afternoon teas' and a meeting to protest against the Licensing Bill of 1908. Opposite below: the Two Brewers, 40 Scotland Green, Tottenham, owed its name to the fact that its custom was also shared by a London and a Burton brewer.

Above: the Fox, Lower Tooting, photographed at a time when it was still thought unnecessary to advertise any beer except 'Entire' outside this modest public house. Even so, porter's share of the London market had fallen from three-quarters in 1863 to one quarter by 1899, when a parliamentary committee was told: 'the ordinary consumer . . . is not satisfied with beer unless it is

bright and clear, carries a good head and is free from acid. He is not satisfied now with porter in pewter pots, but drinks ale in a glass vessel, the contents of which he can see for himself'. Mild ale, sweeter and lighter, took over as the favourite drink of manual workers in London. It sold for 4d a quart in public bars, so acquiring the nickname 'four ale' that survives in the term 'four ale bar', much as porter is obscurely commemorated by 'porterhouse steak'. The characteristic drink of the saloon bar was bitter, the draught counterpart of bottled pale ale. A few brands of draught bitter enjoyed considerable prestige, as indicated by one of the copper panels, above, fixed to the external wall of the Black Friar, Queen Victoria Street, City of London. This public house stands on a site occupied in medieval times by the Dominican Order: hence its name and the reason why the monastic tradition of brewing was the subject of a remarkable scheme of redecoration carried out c. 1905. As the rhyme has it, 'the Abbot of Burton brewed **good ale'. So he may be regarded as the originator of the local skills that helped to shape the reputation of Worthington and other Burton beers.**

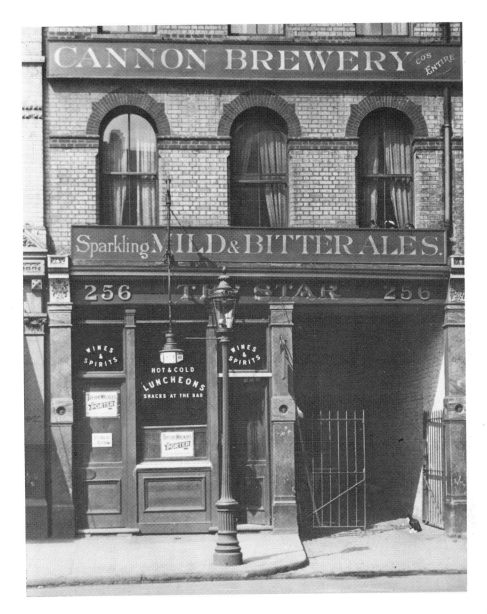

Opposite: the Wheatsheaf, 25 Rathbone Place, Soho, photographed a few years after the Watney Combe Reid merger of 1898 had arranged the triple flow of Reid's stout, Combe's mild and Watney's fine ales to London's largest chain of tied houses. Changes in taste, combined with the inflated prices of licensed property, had been factors in the amalgamation. The revolution had still some way to go when the Star, 256 Borough High Street, Southwark, above, advertised the brewery's 'Entire' on its upper signboard, and porter on the window cards, but gave far greater prominence to 'Sparkling Mild & Bitter Ales'. This period piece was demolished c. 1932. About twenty years later, I remember seeing the word 'Entire' incised on the parapet of a public house, a few miles out of Liverpool Street Station.

31

This is one of the places where I used to spend
my money. It was the sign of "The Angel,"
but it was a fallen angel!

Above: the London Spa, Exmouth Street, Clerkenwell, as it looked in the 1850s. The owner, James Wilson, describes himself on the fascia as 'Importer of and Dealer in Foreign Wines and Spirits'. There is a display of bottles in the shop window on the right. A 'presentation annual' issued at Christmas 1855 by Robert Davey of the Flint Tavern, Hoxton, lists 'strong whisky (over proof)' at 3s 6d (17½p) per bottle, 'fine Scotch' and sherry at 2s (10p) per pint and gin at 1s. The price of Bass's India Pale Ale was 8s (40p) and Guinness's Dublin Stout 7s (35p) per dozen quart bottles. Robert Wood, of the Albion Hotel, Epsom, advertised price reductions in 1861, when he charged, per dozen bottles, 72s (£3.60) for Moët champagne; and per proof gallon, 25s (£1.25) for Martell brandy, pale or brown; 21s (£1.05) for Scotch whisky; 16s (80p) for Jamaica rum; 18s (90p) for Hollands and Schiedam gin, and 12s (60p) for 'mixing' gin.

Several names were applied to public houses which traded mainly in spirits. 'The Gin Shop' is the title of the propagandist leaflet from which Cruikshank's drawing, opposite, is reproduced. 'Spirit house' was the name used in the trade, and 'spirit stores' the words often inscribed on the fascia. 'Shop' and 'stores' did not imply, as they would today, that there was no licence to sell for consumption on the premises. The point is made manifest, in this instance, by the word 'Bar' at the entrance. Spring doors were a characteristic feature of gin-palaces. 'The doors of these splendid dens', Wakefield noted, 'are carefully hung so as to fly open with a touch and shut in an instant'— a matter of some importance, in rough districts, to publicans and their bouncers.

33

Above: the York Minster, 49 Dean Street, Soho, photographed in the 1900s, when its ground floor was fitted out to look like a wine merchant's shop-front, perhaps on account of its location in London's foreign restaurant quarter; just in case any casual custom might be lost, a notice points to 'saloon and private bars'. The off-licence trade in bottled wines and spirits derives, in its modern form, from the Refreshment Houses Act, 1860, which allowed shopkeepers to take out excise licences for the retail sale of wine in bottles without the need to apply for a justices' licence. This was one of a series of measures instigated by Gladstone in the interest of creating free trade in wine and of encouraging its sale: a combination which he believed to be conducive to national

sobriety. In his budget of 1860, he had reduced the duties on wine in response to pressure from Cobden, who was negotiating a trade treaty in Paris and needed a quid pro quo to compensate the French for reducing the tariffs on British manufactured goods. As the result of Gladstone's policies, Gilbeys pioneered the national distribution of wine and the licensed grocer came into being, foreshadowing the growth of the chains of off-licence shops which eventually devoured the trade of the local wine merchants. The middle classes were able to buy wine more cheaply, but the working class frustrated Gladstone's aims by continuing to prefer gin and beer to claret and burgundy.

Above: the Stepney Stores, Bridge Street, Mile End, offered in the 1900s 'sparkling bitter' at 5d per quart, 'our noted porter' at 3d 'in your own jugs', and stout at 4d. The window space is filled with bottles of various beers, backed with a double row of soda-water siphons and fronted with advertisements for two brands of Scotch whisky and one of Irish; there is no evidence of demand for any sort of wine. Gladstone, ironically enough, is the putative father of the modern Scotch whisky business; because it was a Customs & Excise concession, granted in 1860, to blend whiskies from different distilleries in bond, that favoured the emergence of light-bodied, reasonably-priced brands of blended Scotch whisky in bottle. The growth of a mass market for this product is said to have begun when the Franco-Prussian war created boom conditions in Scotland's iron and steel industries. Miners and steelworkers consequently enjoyed good wages throughout the 1870s and sales of blended Scotch whisky increased substantially in the Lowlands. The blending houses started to develop the London market in the 1880s, with such success that Irish whiskey went slowly out of favour. 'Proprietary brands' of Scotch, bottled under the blender's label as a guarantee of quality, were making good headway in the 1890s, when they cost 3s 6d (17½p) a bottle, as readers of that major social document, *The Diary of a Nobody*, may remember.

35

EATING OUT

Pre-Victorian England observed a fairly sharp distinction, in name and function, between inns, which provided accommodation for travellers; taverns, where one might dine and wine; ale-houses, which sold beer, and gin-shops, which sold spirits. These types of establishment corresponded to the modern hotel, restaurant and public house, but only approximately, since the change of name was accompanied to some extent by a reformation of function. The earliest 'hotels' in the West End of London were opened during the Napoleonic wars as small, elegant establishments for well-to-do officers on leave. As the term perhaps implies, the cooking was French, being often done, or supervised, by French refugees. By the 1830s, the word 'hotel' had been appropriated by almost all coaching inns with any claim to first-class status in London, passing as a matter of course to their palatial successors in the railway age. The 'tavern' was another victim of the West End's gastronomic vassalage to Paris. 'Cafés', followed by 'restaurants', provided exotic alternatives to the heavy English fare and, more daring still, pioneered the admittance of women.

The author of *London at Dinner*, 1858, lamented 'the difficulty of finding an Hotel or Restaurant where strangers of the gentler sex may be taken to dine. It is true that, since our intercourse with the Continent, some coffee rooms have opened where gentlemen may take their wives and daughters; but it has not yet become a recognised custom'. Other women set a more difficult problem. They might be dined, at vast expense, in private rooms at the Albion or London Taverns; but it was only at the riverside resorts, Blackwall, Greenwich, Richmond, Hampton Court and Windsor, that 'ladies are to be found as in the Parisian Cafés'. The attraction of Blackwall and Greenwich was the excellence of the fish dinners. Whitebait, the local speciality, abounded in the lower Thames from April to August. Heavily seasoned with cayenne pepper and flavoured with lemon juice, it was accounted a great delicacy; and almost to the end of the century gastronomes paid handsomely for the privilege of eating it, freshly cooked, at the waterside taverns.

Below: the Ship Hotel, Greenwich, designed by Philip Hardwick, surveyor to Greenwich Hospital, and his son P. C. Hardwick, had just

opened for business when this view was engraved in 1857. The Ship enjoyed a position of commercial advantage immediately above the stairs where, as the picture shows, passengers disembarked from the steamboats. Its balconies were said to provide the finest views of Greenwich Reach. Above: 'Greenwich in the Season', a plate from Gustave Doré's *London: A Pilgrimage*, 1872, conveys a sense of the animation of the guests, the excitement of the view from the balconies on a warm summer's night, the brilliance of the gas-lighting reflected in the water, contrasted with the immobility of the stars and of the great ship anchored in midstream.

Above: 'The Greenwich Dinner', by John Leech, appeared in *Punch* for 10 July 1853. This institution received more respectful treatment from a contributor to *All the Year Round* ten years later. The reference, thinly disguised, is to the Ship:

From the 1st of April to the 30th of September, Pleasure's business is in full swing here, and never allows the smallest relaxation. With a view to such business, and nothing else, the Vessel was built; on the heading of its bills it calls itself an hotel, but . . . you will never find rows of boots with number-chalked soles standing outside its chamber-doors, nor regiments of bed-candlesticks on its hall table; no 'boots' lurks up its stairs at the chilly hours of the morning to call anyone who is going by the first train, nor has such a thing as a 'breakfast order' ever been heard within its capacious walls. From its cellar to its attic the Vessel means dinner, and nothing but dinner. On its ground floor are its hall, a lavatory, and the coffee-room with its numbered tables and its cheery look-out on the river. On the first floor are the large rooms used for city companies, testimonial

dinners, and such like, at which between two and three hundred guests often sit down simultaneously; above, are the smaller rooms used for private parties.

The leading establishments in Greenwich were the Ship, the Trafalgar and the Crown & Sceptre: 'all three good but not cheap' in the judgement of Karl Baedeker's handbook to London, 1866. One or other of these set the scene for the 'Ministerial whitebait dinner' held to celebrate the prorogation of Parliament for the summer recess, a date which fell at the peak of the whitebait season. This public junketing came in for a good deal of speculation, disguised as comment, in the press. Leech's cartoon, opposite, from *Punch*, 18 August 1855, sets its sights on identifiable big game: Lord Panmure, Secretary of State for War, on the left, and Lord Palmerston, the Prime Minister. The satire is misplaced, because Palmerston, although certainly no angel, drank very little wine at any time of his life, even if, in his eighty-first year, he once started the day with mutton-chops and port, expressing surprise that he had not discovered earlier what an excellent breakfast it made.

THE MINISTERIAL WHITEBAIT DINNER.—IN VINO VERITAS.

The Hawke Room at the Trafalgar Tavern has been identified as the model for 'Dinner down the River', drawn by Richard Doyle and engraved on wood by the Dalziell Brothers. It is repro- duced, above, from the *Cornhill Magazine* for January 1862. Greenwich diners, according to *All the Year Round*, preferred punch, sherry and nearly always champagne with the dinner. 'After

dinner, by men of the present generation, and at parties where ladies are present, claret is generally drunk; but at the great feeds of the City companies, at the testimonial presentation dinners, at the gatherings of eccentrically-named clubs—institutions with a superstructure of indulgence springing from a substratum of charity—nothing but East India brown sherry and sound port'.

The *Nouveau Guide à Londres*, published by Chaix for visitors to the Great Exhibition of 1851, warned them not to expect the equivalent of Parisian restaurants. 'Dining rooms', of which there were at least 250, open from 1 pm to 6 pm, catered for people of modest means, providing cuts off the joint, vegetables and bread, for 1s (5p). Even Simpson's fish restaurant near Billingsgate, 'with an almost European reputation', charged only 1s 6d (7½p) for its table d'hôte. A pint of stout or old ale cost 4d to 5d, porter or ale 3d; water and table beer ('differing only in the colour') were free. Eating shops ('corresponding to the buffets of railway stations in France') were commonest in the main streets of the City. These supplied cold meats, pastries and buns in variety, sometimes fruit, and assorted cordials. Above: a drawing of 'Dining Rooms in Bucklersbury', by William McConnell, from Sala's *Twice Round the Clock in London*, 1859. 'Hundreds upon hundreds of City clerks', according to Sala,

> consume an orthodox dinner of meat, vegetables and cheese—and on high days and holidays pudding—at one p.m. Their numbers are sufficient to cram almost to suffocation the eating-houses of Cheapside, the Poultry, Mark Lane, Cornhill and especially Cheapside. Of late years there has been an attempt to change the eating-houses of Cheapside into pseudo 'restaurants'. Seductive announcements, brilliantly emblazoned, and showily framed and glazed, have been hung up, relating to 'turtle' and 'venison'; salmon, with wide waddling mouths, have gasped in the windows; and insinuating mural inscriptions have hinted at the existence of 'Private dining rooms for ladies'. Now, whatever can ladies—though I have the

authority of Dibdin and my own lips for declaring that there are fine ones in the city—want to come and dine in Cheapside for? At these restaurants they give you things with French names, charge you a stated sum for attendance, provide the pale ale in silver tankards, and take care of your hat and coat; but I like them not—neither, I believe, do my friends, the one-o'clock-dining clerks.

Clerks, in this period, took their main meal in the middle of the day and called it dinner; but their principals, who dined in the evening, went out to luncheon. This was now quite a substantial meal, instead of a glass of sherry and a biscuit, partly because the dinner hour was later. Below: a 'silhouette' drawing by William Brunton illustrates an article in *London Society* for March 1870:

The West End luncheon bars have, I think, made a considerable improvement of late years. They cannot indeed cook a mutton-chop or a beefsteak. That interesting branch of the fine arts has never flourished west of Temple Bar. But they can do most other things very well. You can take ladies with you to Verey's, in Regent Street, and they will stop in their carriages and do their own very satisfactory luncheons in Oxford Street and elsewhere. I think Spiers and Pond deserve well of the community for the good luncheon purposes to which they have applied their Australian experiences. But you always lunch in a hurry at a buffet, expecting the whistle of your train. The Regent Street bars are extremely good. . . . At the corner of Burlington Street the Messrs. Blanchard have one of the best possible luncheon bars. You stand, indeed, and the whole place is rather crowded; we hope to see it enlarged. But the system is excellent, the viands are good, and you may make any number of observations, if you are so inclined, on life and character. You also get that variety on which I must insist as essential to a well-planned luncheon bar.

Brunton, by taking his view from the back of the bar counter, enables us to grasp the variety of the drinks, if not of the victuals. Between the beer engine on the left, and the tiny cask of sherry or port on the right, there are two decanters of wine, and an urn containing coffee, or possibly tea.

In 1860, a man about town recollected in the Nineties, 'there were very few restaurants of any importance in London. Spiers and Pond had not yet come from Australia to turn the tavern and the public house into a smart rendezvous, with counters, glasses and pretty girls coquettishly dressed. The old tavern and chop-house life had not been obliterated'. Some of the older establishments trimmed their sails to the wind of change; others ignored it. Baedeker, in 1866, singled out Simpson's in the Strand as a large, well-appointed establishment (*grosses schönes Lokal mit eleganter Einrichtung*) where the ordinary dinner of joint, vegetables and cheese, 'tip-top' (*recht gut*), cost 2s 6d (12½p) and a pint of ale 6d (2½p). There were separate dining rooms for ladies at the London, 191 Fleet Street (*gutes Haus*) where the ordinary

dinner, of five or six courses, cost 2s 9d (14p); but the Cock, 201 Fleet Street, ('known for good chops and steaks') was for men only.

The concept of the restaurant, as the foreign origin of the word implies, is not native to England. So it was hardly fortuitous that early examples of the genre emerged under French or Italian names: Gatti's and the Café Royal in 1863, Kettner's in 1867 and Pagani's in 1871. Such restaurants, unlike the old-fashioned chop-houses, offered a variety of dishes à la carte. Among the West End restaurants awarded a star by Baedeker in 1879 were old-established houses (Evans's, Simpson's), new ones trading, so to speak, under foreign flags (Blanchard's, Kettner's), parts of the Spiers and Pond catering empire (the Criterion, the Gaiety) and the Holborn Restaurant, 218 High

Holborn. An advertisement for the last of these claimed in that year 'the attractions of the Chief Parisian Establishments with the quiet and order essential to English customs' and assured ladies that they could enter the dining saloon 'without passing the public buffet'. No doubt the contemporary Lincoln's Inn Buffet, shown on page 60, which looks like a resort of drinking men, was meant. The marbled and mirrored Holborn Buffet, opposite, a rather too grand luncheon bar, contrasts with the grill room of a City public house, the Daniel Lambert, Ludgate Circus, below, drawn by G. K. Jones for the *Daily Graphic*, 10 September 1891. In the chop-house and tavern tradition, fresh meat is laid out for the customer's selection, and cooked on a grill in his presence. The bar, as in the preceding pictures, is in the charge of barmaids. These young women were already the subject of popular mythology. 'Keep away from barmaids', Arthur Roberts used to implore music-hall audiences, 'whose attraction

every charm aids'. A reporter investigating 'The Barmaid's Lot' in 1895, concluded that the supposed sirens were

> a very much misunderstood class of woman. To the ordinary mind, barmaids are bright, rather flashy-looking women who will serve beer and chaff, or split Scotch and repartee, to any man who pays the price at a public bar. They are always cheerful, have a word and a smile for everyone, and have a decided penchant for 'peroxide' hair and painted cheeks. The result is that their morals are considered elastic, if not lax, and they are submitted to both temptation and insult.

The first issue of the *Daily Mail*, on 4 May 1896, took a short, sharp view of the matter: 'These unhappy creatures are kept at work from seven in the morning till one or two the next morning, a daily toil of eighteen to nineteen hours' labour. Aversion to domestic service is really at the bottom of this scandal'.

The antiquarian J. C. Timbs, recollecting in 1866 'many changes in matters concerning whitebait at Greenwich', compared the unpretentious weatherboarded taverns of his youth with 'the handsome architectural piles . . . erected in their places'. These, forty years later, had reverted to public house status. Above: the Trafalgar Tavern, Greenwich, 1837, designed by Joseph Kay, surveyor of Greenwich Hospital. It ceased trading in 1915 and was successively used as the Royal Alfred Aged Merchant Seamen's Institute, a working men's club and a block of flats. The photograph was taken in 1965, when it was restored and relicensed.

The whitebait taverns enjoyed a long run of success. The compiler of Murray's *Handbook for*

Kent noted in the revised edition of 1892 that the parties who came from London to dine at Greenwich had 'greatly decreased in numbers and importance now that whitebait can be procured as fresh in the London shops as here'. James Payn, two years later, marvelled that anybody had ever travelled to Greenwich at all 'by one of the worst railways or one of the ugliest roads in England'. The river trip he thought 'very pleasant in summer time, though rather tedious, especially as regards the return journey, but one must be young and strong for such violent delights. I am told, however, that even our gilt youth no longer go to Greenwich; the tramways have made the road impassible for their four-in-hands, and the place has not the same attractions'. The 1889 edition of Baedeker describes the Ship and the Trafalgar as 'both very expensive' and the 1900 edition no longer mentions the Trafalgar or the Crown & Sceptre. In 1908 the Ship closed down for gastronomic purposes. The growth in the number and variety of restaurants in the West End may have been the decisive factor that made the whitebait taverns uncompetitive. There were few captive markets of any size outside the City and the West End. Suburban restaurants needed a *raison d'être* and probably had to be content with a mainly seasonal trade. One of these was the Star & Garter, Putney, photographed, below, on a serene day in 1881 when time seems to have stopped. This part of the river, according to Thorne's *Environs of London*, 1876, 'is the headquarters of Thames boating men. It was the starting-place for the Thames regatta in its palmy days; and it is now, as everybody knows, the starting-place in the Oxford and Cambridge boat-race. The crews take up their abode at Putney, at the Star and Garter, or at a private house, during their preparatory trials and coaching'.

Mr. Slinn provided 'dinners and old wines' for relatively affluent customers. A cheaper, simpler bill of fare would have been available at the adjoining Refreshment Rooms.

GOING OUT

Pleasure grounds, theatres and taverns were the main places of public recreation for Londoners well into Victorian times. The differences between them were not sharply defined. Musical entertainments were given in public houses; theatres supplied excisable liquor, and pleasure gardens were often laid out in the grounds of suburban taverns. Most of the pleasure gardens on the northern outskirts were the resort of respectable citizens who came *en famille* on Sundays, less often on summer evenings, to enjoy the pleasures of eating and drinking, or to play cricket and bowls, in countrified surroundings. The grounds on the Surrey side of the Thames offered participation in rougher sports. The activities at the Red House, Battersea, below, were described in retrospect by Thomas Kirk in the *London City Mission Magazine* for September 1870:

That which made this part of Battersea Fields so notorious was the gaming, sporting and pleasure-grounds at the 'Red House' and 'Balloon' public houses, and Sunday fairs, held throughout the summer months. These have been the resort of hundreds and thousands, from royalty and nobility down to the poorest pauper and the meanest beggar. And surely if ever there was a place out of hell that surpassed Sodom and Gomorrah in ungodliness and abomination, this was it. Here the worst men and vilest of the human race seemed to try to outvie each other in wicked deeds. I have gone to this sad spot on the afternoon and evening of the Lord's day, when there have been from 60 to 120 horses and donkeys racing, foot-racing, walking matches, flying boats, flying horses, roundabouts, theatres, comic actors, shameless

dancers, conjurers, fortune-tellers, gamblers of every description, drinking-booths, stalls, hawkers and vendors of all kinds of articles. It would take a more graphic pen than mine to describe the mingled shouts and noises and the unmentionable doings of this pandemonium on earth.

Frith might have done justice to the scene with a painting to match 'Ramsgate Sands' and 'Derby Day'.

The success of Sabbatarian campaigns to close other places of recreation left public houses without much competition. For ordinary people, there was nowhere else to go, and licensed victuallers in early Victorian times displayed much versatility as purveyors of amusement. The entertainments offered in the London of the 1840s ranged from promenade concerts, held at the Crown & Anchor in the Strand, to evenings of music and song in which the customers participated, and did not exclude the coarser spectacles surviving from an earlier age. 'Ratting' became the main indoor blood-sport after cock-fighting, or at least the holding of mains in public, was made unlawful in 1849. It was enjoyed by high as well as low society, as the view of a rat-pit at a public house, above, reproduced from Mayhew's *Life and Labour of the London Poor*, clearly indicates. Some of the spectators hold tankards and others stop-watches. 'Rat-killing Legers', in which dogs were matched to kill a given number in the shortest time, were still held at public houses in Birmingham and the Black Country in the early 1900s.

49

The early music halls were almost invariably the offshoots of public houses that offered customers the means of convivial eating and drinking accompanied by a programme of entertainment. One of the most successful was the Eagle, City Road, Shoreditch. Above is a representation of its pleasure grounds. Variety and vaudeville shows were given in the Rotunda (background) or in the Moorish Pavilion, and dancing and singing took place in the open air, where tables were laid out with refreshments. 'Taverns of this description', Peter Cunningham's *Handbook for London* commented in 1849, 'have seriously injured the minor theatres, as at houses like the Eagle, with both music and a spirit licence, people can see, hear and drink'. Under the Theatres Act, 1843, theatres licensed for drama lost, but variety theatres retained, the right to serve drinks in the auditorium. So corks no longer popped in the Grecian Theatre, the successor to the Moorish Pavilion, after the new owner, Robert Conquest, took out a full licence for drama in 1851. He built a gigantic ballroom platform in the grounds, and introduced fancy-dress dances, which got the place a name for immorality. In 1882, when the theatre and pleasure gardens failed commercially, General Booth bought the site for a Salvation Army citadel. He was compelled by the terms of the lease to keep the Eagle Tavern open, until it too was pulled down in 1899. It survives in the familiar rhyme:

Up and down the City Road,
In and out the Eagle,
That's the way the money goes—
Pop goes the weasel!

Below: John Tenniel's drawing illustrates a passage in *The Gordian Knot*:

It would not have occurred to you, passing a squalid-looking public house, very scantily illuminated, and in miserable contrast with the flare, and plate-glass, and gigantic vats of the Gin-Vatican opposite, that by going past a singularly dirty bar, and paying a very small deposit, you would make your way into a temple of the drama. . . . It was a real theatre, low, small, and rickety, and flavoured with various liquid odours, as Milton says, besides the dominant scent of the strongest tobacco. Good stout benches, with backs, and with flaps to hold the metallic or ceramic vase (glass was little affected) held a coarse, but not particularly vicious-looking audience. The unskilled mechanic came here, while his superior, the skilled workman, frequented the music hall.

The artistic tradition of the Victorian music-hall derived from the tavern concerts of the eighteenth century, or from the 'saloon theatres' which began to flourish between 1830 and 1840. The Duke's Arms, Stangate Street, Lambeth, supported the Bower Saloon Theatre, housed originally in a Moorish pavilion in its grounds. 'The above delightful and favourite Garden with the entire and extensive ALTERATIONS', a playbill of 9 July 1838 announced, 'has for many a Reason, opened for the Summer Season'. It had an orchestra and stage from the outset, when it presented elaborate dioramas accompanied by music. This policy met with no success. George Hodson, who took over in 1841, did better with programmes of songs, vaudeville and melodrama,

as advertised in the playbill, opposite. Music halls gained an increasing share of the market as the pleasure grounds and garden taverns succumbed to the outward march of London, and as the 'legitimate theatre' abandoned variety entertainment after the Act of 1843. There were twenty-three music halls in London by the early 1860s. Some of these failed, or burned down, to be succeeded by larger and more elaborate theatres, no longer annexed to taverns. A parliamentary committee reported in 1892 that London's thirty-five major music halls entertained 45,000 people nightly, and that the five largest had audiences of 2,000 each. One of the casualties was the Bower Theatre at the Duke's Arms. The *Illustrated Sporting and Dramatic News* for 20 October 1877 celebrated its end with a drawing, 'The Last of the Bower', above, and a valedictory appreciation:

Many an aspiring histrionic amateur has trodden its boards, for although a mere band-box of a theatre, it had an excellent and roomy stage. Ah! how many glowing aspirations for the future has the Bower hissed and jeered into oblivion; how many a stage-struck youth and maiden there found themselves mistaken in their vocation. . . . Yet the Bower introduced many a good actor to his profession, and our Westminster Road playgoers can yet remember the glories of 1840, when the Bower Saloon boasted a good company, well-painted scenery, excellent properties and costumes, and better still, a nightly, if not silent, audience.

BREAKING OUT

A public house is not, or ought not to be, just a retail outlet for a manufacturer's products. As it is primarily a place of refreshment and recreation, it follows that this function should be expressed in its architectural form. A 'Picturesque' manner was sometimes thought appropriate for residential areas in the 1830s and 1840s. Below: the Castle, Ross-on-Wye, Herefordshire, Tudoresque, with romantic gables and bargeboards. It dates from 1838. A more exotic type of picturesque building, the 'Swiss cottage', illustrated in P. F. Robinson's *Rural Architecture*, 1822, and in his *Designs for*

Ornamental Villas, 1827, caught the general fancy. In 1854 Prince Albert had a full-sized chalet brought in sections from Switzerland and erected in the grounds of Osborne, where his children were taught carpentry or cookery and entertained visitors to tea. The public had an opportunity of using models made from more durable materials.

Opposite above: the Swiss Cottage, Finchley Road, Hampstead, opened by Francis Redmond c. 1840. The picture is dated by the figure on the extreme left carrying an advertisement for the *Pictorial Times*, which ran from 1844 to 1848. His

presence, with that of the apple-women and the baked-potato man, indicate the commercial potential of the site, enhanced in 1856, when it became the northern terminus of the General Omnibus Company's line to London Bridge, and in 1868, when an Underground railway station was opened as 'Swiss Cottage'. Below: a contemporary counterpart in south London, the Swiss Cottage, 149 Stanstead Road, Forest Hill; once a semi-rural resort, it now faces an arterial road.

Opposite: a drawing by John Leech, from *Punch*, 1860. By this date the back-fitting and the counter were occasionally installed in the middle of a large public room to form an 'island bar', ringed with a number of 'compartments' like that illustrated by George du Maurier, above, also from *Punch*, 1879. The Eagle, City Road, when it was put up for sale in 1887, had 'a commodious liquor shop', six entrances, and five compartments; other houses had as many as eight.

Although du Maurier's barmaid is concerned about the condition of the customer on the right, Leech's characters pay no attention to the small children sampling the jug of beer they have been sent to fetch. There was wide acceptance of beer as a normal part of everyone's diet in an age when water and milk were too often infected. Thus seven gallons were supplied in 1853 for a Wesleyan Sunday School Children's Treat by a publican in High Wycombe. *Every Boy's Book of Sports and Amusements*, first published in 1856, recommended it for breakfast: 'Tea we believe to be undesirable, and a pint of really sound bitter will be found to agree much better'. Schoolboys at Christ's Hospital and Marlborough drank beer for breakfast in the 1860s, and at Bradfield to the end of the century; older boys at Marlborough and

Rugby had it with supper until about 1914. A better water supply, thanks to 'sanitary reform', and the greater popularity and cheapness of tea and cocoa, were factors in the decay of the practice.

The Victorians were accustomed, if not reconciled, to the sight of children on licensed premises. Parliament took no action to protect minors until the Licensing Act, 1872, disallowed the sale of spirits 'for consumption on the premises' to any person apparently under the age of sixteen. Twentieth-century legislators have done their best to make up for the laissez-faire policy of their predecessors. The 'Child Messenger' Act of 1901 prohibited the sale of 'intoxicating liquor', except in corked and sealed containers, to children under fourteen. It was not until 1923 that the law set out to prevent the sale or purchase of 'intoxicants' to or by persons under eighteen, the consumption of 'intoxicants' by them in bars, and the purchase of drink on their behalf in bars by adults. However, beer, porter, cider and perry (but not wine) might lawfully be sold to persons aged sixteen and above for consumption with a meal served in a part of the building which was not a bar. A bar was grimly defined as any part of the premises 'mainly or exclusively used for the sale and consumption of alcoholic liquor'.

57

Most of the urban public houses built in the 1850s wore the sober uniform of the Italian style, adapted to commercial needs. The Balmoral Castle, Churchill Gardens Estate, Pimlico, opposite, was built in the year when the Queen's Highland residence was completed, 1856. A hundred years later, Westminster City Council and their architects Powell and Moya made the enlightened decision to preserve it when the surrounding area was cleared for a great new housing estate. The White Horse, Market Road, Islington, above, is one of five public houses and two hotels designed between 1850 and 1855 by J. B. Bunning, architect to the Corporation of London, to serve the new Metropolitan (or 'Caledonian') Cattle Market. They are similar in character, except that the hotels, two bays wider, are even more monumental: 'large, roomy and substantial buildings', according to *The Leisure Hour*, 1856, 'calculated for the accommodation of many hundreds. . . . Everything connected with the market has been designed with a view to strength and permanency, not without such ornament as becomes the structure of a wealthy community. . . .' The Market, nevertheless, was a commercial failure. The hotels, the City Arms and the Queen's Arms, had been turned into tenements by 1873; they are still there, with three more of Bunning's public houses, the Lion, the Lamb and the Butchers Arms.

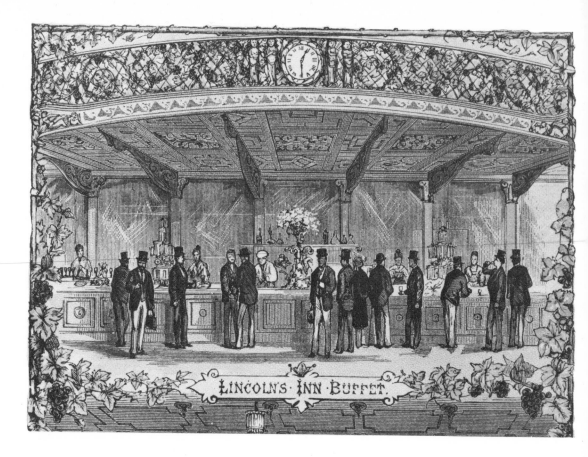

LINCOLN'S INN BUFFET.

In the 1850s, the Gothic Revival entered its second phase. The growth of the railways made available, at low cost, building materials of many different types and colours. These were combined to achieve rich decorative effects, with the help of details adopted from Italian, French and Flemish architecture. The sacred texts of the movement were *The Stones of Venice* and other books by Ruskin. He was driven to fury by the corruption of his ideas. 'I have had *in*direct influence', he wrote to the *Pall Mall Gazette* on 16 March 1872, 'on nearly every cheap villa-builder between [Denmark Hill] and Bromley; and there is scarcely a public house near the Crystal Palace but sells its gin-and-bitters under pseudo-Venetian capitals copied from the Church of the

Madonna of Health or of Miracles'. These fruits of the Gothic Revival included some robust examples of popular architecture. The Holborn Restaurant survived long enough to allow Sir Nikolaus Pevsner to admire 'fine displays of mosaic and majolica' in its Lincoln's Inn Buffet, above, which dated from c. 1877. Bizarre combinations of styles were characteristic of the architecture of entertainment—theatres, music halls, restaurants and public houses. The King Lud, Ludgate Circus, opposite, drawn for *The Builder* of 1 April 1871, was built of Portland stone and white Suffolk brick, with polished columns of Aberdeen granite framing the ground-floor windows. The architect was Lewis Isaacs and the cost £5,000.

Attention may be attracted to the whole elevation, or concentrated on the ground-floor front, as in the Old Fountain, 36 Broadway, Deptford, above. Such fronts are sometimes later additions by improving landlords. This one, with agreeably arcaded doors and windows, has a decidedly liquorish flavour. At the Horse Shoe, Tottenham Court Road, Holborn, opposite, the *tout ensemble* dominates, and no wonder. This free-wheeling, or free-skidding, exercise in the Second Empire style dates from 1875, except for the addition on the right. E. L. Paraire was the architect. The ground floor originally contained a grill room, a luncheon bar, a large café and an estaminet where, it was claimed, the latest suppers and the earliest breakfasts in the West End were served. There were 'dining rooms for both sexes' on the first floor, listed by Baedeker in 1879: 'table d'hôte, 5.30 to 8.30 pm, 3s 6d' (17½p). A friendly journalist described the Wine Shades as 'a charming little retreat in which huge vats of wines and spirits are embowered with ferns and flowers'. The basement also accommodated a billiard room and 'a vast horse-shoe bar' where the central feature was 'a rippling fountain which plashes and sparkles amidst bright green foliage'. An American bar was added in the 1880s. This photograph must have been taken in 1925, when Noel Coward's *The Vortex*, advertised on the open-top bus, was running at the Little Theatre.

APOGEE

Thomas Hughes, preaching in 1879, nearly anticipated Thorstein Veblen's theory of conspicuous consumption: 'The standard of expenditure has been increasing by leaps and bounds, and demoralising trade, society, every industry, and every profession, until a false ideal has established itself, and the aim of life is too commonly to get, not to be, while men are valued more and more for what they have, not for what they are'. Acquisition and competition were compelling motives in the last quarter of the century. At home, the wage-earner's purchasing power was extended by a steady increase in real wages in the face of falling retail prices. Overseas, the proclamation of the Queen as Empress of India inaugurated the era of imperial expansion. So it is not surprising to find a spirit of self-confidence reflected in the buildings of the period. The architecture and interior decoration of public houses in the 1880s express an uninhibited love of display and a restless energy that compels every surface to be decorated and every detail to be elaborated. Opposite: the Crown Liquor Saloon, Queen Victoria Street, Belfast, faces the main-line railway terminus. The powerful, red and yellow pattern of the ceiling, the gilded pillars and Corinthian capitals, the heraldic lions and griffins marking the entrances to panelled 'snugs', private as an eighteenth-century squire's box pew, the long, marble-topped counter divided by carved oak screens, the lettering, the arched recesses, and the decorated tiles on the floor, all contribute to the richness and splendour of an integrated plan of decoration.

Below: nightfall at the Red Lion, Duke of York Street, St James's Square, Westminster. The ground floor of this otherwise unremarkable early nineteenth-century building was refitted to create three small but splendid late Victorian bars, the finest to survive in the West End, pages 68-9.

Murray's *Handbook for Travellers in Ireland*, 1866, noted 'the beautiful examples of decorative architecture displayed so largely in its public buildings' among the things likely to surprise and please visitors to Belfast, 'a city of essentially modern growth and appearance'. Its commercial buildings, too, reflect the upswing of enterprise and prosperity in this late-developing Victorian city. Above: the Bee-Hive, 193 Falls Road, Belfast. Delight in broken surfaces embraces everything from the well-conceived sign to the daring High Baroque conception of building out windows from recesses.

Opposite: the saloon bar of the Leicester, New Coventry Street, Westminster, photographed in 1895. Huge mirrors, set in a framework of mahogany panels and pilasters, reflect the bar counter on the left and the otherwise invisible back-fitting, creating an illusion of greater spaciousness. The use of large, thick sheets of polished glass was greatly extended by James Chance's invention of 'patent plate' in 1838. One of the first customers was Joseph Paxton who applied it to glazing the conservatory at Chatsworth, and later at the Crystal Palace. Plate-glass was intrinsically suited to display and therefore for use in the windows of shops and public houses. The popularity of large looking-glasses came in with the Exhibition of 1862, when mirror-glass was fitted into many types of furniture, especially sideboards. A large mirror in a carved and gilded frame, fixed above the fire-place, was Alice's point of departure in *Through the Looking-Glass*, 1871.

Above: A late Victorian interior at the Red Lion, Duke of York Street, St James's Square, Westminster. This small building exemplifies the three qualities postulated by Mr J. M. Richards as 'essential to real pub character: dark rich colours to give an effect of warmth and cosiness; the breaking-up of the plan into small, distinct areas to give an effect of intimacy and enclosure and richness of texture to give a sense of plenty and well-being'. The second part of this formula does not inspire much enthusiasm among the magistrates. They are more interested in ensuring 'overall supervision' by the publican as a safeguard against the commission of misdemeanours

punishable under the licensing laws. The owners also seem to favour open spaces to accommodate the crush at peak hours of service. So it will probably become increasingly difficult to find Victorian public houses in so fine a state of preservation as the Red Lion.

Professor Henry-Russell Hitchcock has suggested that the fittings designed c. 1858 by Alfred Stevens for the dining-room at Dorchester House, Park Lane, 'with their carved mahogany frames, cut and engraved mirrors, and aedicular construction . . . could well have been the inspiration for the lush decoration characteristic of later Victorian gin-palace interiors'. The technological

cause of this efflorescence of decorated glass is indicated by the words of a monograph published in 1871:

> Now that such vast improvements have been made in the manufacture of plate-glass, and it may readily be procured in large dimensions and thickness, at a comparatively moderate cost, the decorator has bestowed much attention upon it; and the result has been the introduction of the art of glass embossing and writing in burnished gold. . . . Within the last few years it has been brought to a marvellous state of development; and its superiority over any other method of surface decoration has led to its very general adoption in the more tastily fitted-up public-house bars of the metropolis, and of the better class of public-houses in the leading provincial towns. It is now no uncommon thing for the inside walls of a richly decorated spirit bar to be entirely covered with glass, either embossed or written on in burnished or matt gold . . .

Examples of 'writing in burnished gold' are reproduced on pages 70-1. The panel at the Red Lion, above, illustrates the combination of the two main processes used in embossing or engraving glass. Brilliant-cutting with a stone wheel produced graceful arabesques, fish-tails and dots that were gilded or highly polished to achieve effects of light and shade. With acid-etching, the more versatile process, any design could be traced on a glass surface after it had been masked with brunswick black to 'resist' the action of the fluoric acid that was then poured over it to etch the design. A third technique, back-painting of glass, was probably used in depicting the figures of swans and flamingoes which can just be identified on page 44.

Opposite, a panel of mirror glass on the bar back-fitting at the Balmoral Castle, Churchill Gardens, Pimlico, inscribed with ornately decorated letters in red and gold, or green and gold, shaded with a black and gold border to make them stand out as if they had been executed in relief. Other panels celebrate Martell and Hennessy cognac and 'Diamond Cream Gin'. Above: gilded letters on a mirror at the Warwick Castle, Maida Vale, advertise another famous branded product. The label on the bottle of Bass's pale ale, first issued in 1855, is the oldest now used in the brewing industry. The design has never been altered and has never dated. It is said to have been the work of a member of Bass's London staff. He chose, as the central feature, the company's shipping mark—a red triangle—and in that moment of inspiration devised one of the world's most familiar trade marks, the first to be registered under the Trade Marks Registration Act of 1875. Another distinction was achieved seven years later, when Manet painted 'A Bar at the Folies-Bergères', in which the bottle is twice represented.

71

The Leicester, New Coventry Street, Westminster, built in 1886-7, was one of many substantial public houses designed by Treadwell & Martin. Their client here, as at the Dover Castle, pages 82-3, was Charles Best & Co. This picture of the first-floor wine bar was taken in 1895 by Bedford Lemere, the leading architectural photographers of the day. Reproduction Louis XV furniture, wall-to-wall carpeting, subdued lighting and the near-nude female figures on the newel-posts are distinguishing marks of an expensive West End bar with a faintly erotic atmosphere.

Wine bars and American bars charged higher prices than the saloon, condescending to serve bottled but not draught beer. They were not synonymous terms. In 1888 the Horse Shoe, Tottenham Court Road, had a 'wine shades', or basement wine and spirit bar, and an American bar on the ground floor which dispensed specialities such as Flash of Lightning, Rattlesnake, Gum Tickler, Eye Duster, Kidney Twist, Liver Syringe, Lung Purifier and Tonsil Tease.

The Assembly House, Kentish Town, above and opposite, was built in 1898, almost seventy years after the earliest gin-palace. This term, applied to late Victorian public houses, is something of a misnomer; they were often tied to brewers, but seldom to distillers, and had no special interest in the sale of gin. The gin-palaces of the 1830s exercised their potent spell through the brilliant illumination of large areas of plain plate-glass. Late Victorian interiors achieve glittering effects of theatrical unreality with arcades of intricately engraved mirrors, set in frames of carved and polished mahogany, and reflecting other mirrors, until the walls seem to recede and space dissolves. The scene is held in balance by the island bar back-fitting, and by the strongly-patterned ceiling.

The earliest embossed wallpapers, Tynecastle and Lincrusta, were developed in the 1870s. Anaglypta, patented in 1887, succeeded Lincrusta as the material most commonly used for decorating ceilings in relief.

Panels of decorated glass from the Assembly House, Kentish Town, above, and from the Salisbury, 90 St Martin's Lane, Westminster, opposite, a building of the same date. The delicate acid-etched design, which varies from one panel to the next, is enclosed in a uniform brilliant-cut frame. The qualities of the two processes are perfectly matched.

At the Salisbury, St Martin's Lane, the designs on the windows, opposite, offer the man in the street a foretaste of the visual delight to be found on the other side. Above: they admit the light without exposing the customers inside to public inspection.

Quasi-sculptural use of mahogany to enclose curved sheets of decorated glass, recessed in an outer framework of stucco and pillars of cast iron, at the Prince Alfred, Formosa Street, Maida Vale, opposite and above. It dates from c. 1863. This part of Maida Vale keeps its Victorian character.

The district, open country until the 1830s and 1840s, takes its name from the Hero of Maida, a local public house. The hero was Sir John Stuart, who gained a decisive victory over a superior French force at the battle of Maida, Calabria, in 1806.

Above: the saloon bar and, opposite, the public bar, of the Dover Castle, Westminster Bridge Road, Lambeth, designed by Treadwell & Martin, and photographed by Bedford Lemere in 1896. They represent different standards of living. The public bar has sawdust on the floor and a brass footrail for perpendicular drinkers where the saloon has Italian mosaic and well-made, buttock-supporting stools. Ten pulls for draught beer compare with one in the superior bar, where the lowest shelf is stacked with bottled beers and the highest with boxes of cigars. Nothing distinguishes the public bar more sharply from its counterpart today than the two tiers of barrels set into the back-fitting. These, like the twenty-two concubines of the Byzantine emperor in Gibbon, are designed for use rather than ostentation. The contents are described on the labels as 'Brandy', 'Old Tom', 'Gin', 'Irish Whisky', 'Special Irish', 'Jamaica Rum', 'Special Scotch', 'Sherry', 'Choice

Old Port', 'Old Scotch Whisky', 'Pale Old Brandy', and so on, without benefit of brand name. Customers who were not prepared to take the quality of these products on trust could demand to be served with a tot straight from the bottle, or at least from the spirit dispenser, the urn-shaped vessel labelled 'Buchanan'. In each bar, as at the Leicester, Buchanan Blend is the most prominently displayed bottle. Scotch whisky takes pride of place, with Greer's Old Vatted Highland represented in the public bar and Roderick Dhu in the saloon, where a wide range of proprietary wines, spirits, liqueurs and cordials is displayed on the back-fitting. One other marked difference between the two bars is apparent. The restaurant adjoining the saloon bar is supplemented by a counter service. 'Mulled claret' and 'soups—always ready' are on offer; a plate of boiled eggs and a jar of 'Scotch eggs' are also visible. In the public bar, there is nothing to eat.

SPECIAL SITUATIONS

Tennyson, bidding the great world to spin for ever down the ringing grooves of change, used the image of the railway track to symbolise the Victorian idea of continuous progress. That is what it must have meant to the brewers of Burton-on-Trent after a spur line to the Midland Railway was built in 1839, and a cheap and rapid means of transport enabled them to distribute their products in the great urban markets. Thirty years after the establishment of the railway link, Burton presented the extraordinary spectacle of a town devoted almost entirely to the production of beer. It had twenty-six breweries, connected with maltings, cooperages and the goods station by seventy-one miles of private railway, crossing the streets at eight points by grace of Parliament. Bass's annual output rose from 10,000 barrels in 1830 to 100,000 in 1850 and had reached almost a million by 1890, by which time Guinness's brewery in Dublin was the largest in the world. Over the same period, hundreds of small local breweries, once they lost the protection from distant competition afforded by high transport costs, went out of business.

The retail side of the drink trade was also deeply affected by social and economic change precipitated by the railway system. People could now travel long distances without suffering from exhaustion and cold, with the consequent need to take restorative action at frequent staging posts. So, as passengers and freight deserted the trunk roads, the trade of the coaching inns declined. Some, like the Talbot, Southwark, shown on page 24, took in parcels for the railways. Their successors were the many-storeyed 'station hotels' in the cities and the 'buffet refreshment bars' and 'railway taverns' built to attract the custom of short-distance passengers. Left: the Three Nuns, 9 Aldgate High Street, City of London, taken from a photo-lithograph in *Building News* for 26 April 1878. Tarring & Wilkinson designed it for the Metropolitan Railway Company as a combined tavern and hotel, with twenty-two bedrooms, *one* bathroom, one public and three private dining-rooms, 'first and second class luncheon and refreshment bars, and public and private bars'. The job, carried out in elevations of red brick and Doulton's terra-cotta, cost £10,000, including £2,000 for the bar-fittings, designed by the architects themselves: cabinet work and partitions of pitch-pine, 'with stained glass in pattern lead lights', counter tops of white marble 'for the first and second class departments' and of

mahogany elsewhere. This by-product of railway company enterprise adjoined Aldgate Underground Station.

The Hampstead Junction Line reached Willesden in 1860, a presage of doom to the woods and fields of unravished Middlesex. 'A very few years ago', Thorne wrote in *The Environs of London*, 1876, 'Willesden was a quiet, retired, thoroughly rural village, a favourite haunt of the holiday-maker, summer rambler, botanist and sketcher, who reckoned on the White Horse for a substantial country lunch or dinner. Now London has reached its outskirts. The builder has invaded the once tranquil meadows; field paths (and fields also) are disappearing; and the lanes are for the most part green no longer'. In 1879 the Metro-

politan Railway reached Willesden Green, where the Spotted Dog, above, photographed about that time, still retained a country air, with its tree-shaded pleasure ground on the right, dove-cotes, a pair of geese, and a troop of goslings marching left. In the centre of the group of figures, the mandatory policeman and a real spotted dog occupy positions appropriate to their symbolic roles. A basket of hay and a pail of water, left, are set ready for the refreshment of horses. There is economic significance in the raised white letters stuck on the ground-floor windows. They spell out the names of 'Younger & Co's Pale & Edinburgh Ales' and of 'Dunville's VR Old Irish Whisky'—commodities probably unknown to the inhabitants before the railway came.

Above: the Railway Bell, Dover Road, Folkestone, looks like a railway building and was probably built by the South-Eastern Railway Company in 1843, when the original Folkestone Station opened. It faced the station yard from the opposite side of Dover Road for a hundred years, until it was wrecked in an air raid. Folkestone was an insignificant fishing town until the railway link to London encouraged harbour improvement, a daily steam packet service to Boulogne and the summer holiday trade.

Opposite above: the Stradbroke Arms, Darsham, Suffolk, faces the entrance to Darsham Station, outside the village, on the London to Lowestoft road. It must have been built shortly after 1854, when the East Suffolk Railway was incorporated. The early Victorian saloon bar has pitch-pine panelling and window-seats, and is separated from the serving space by sliding glazed hatches instead of a counter. There is a Commercial Room. Public houses of this type, in Mr John Piper's words, 'are a part of railway architecture; they help to form a knot of interest round that isolated feature of country building, the railway station; station approaches would be bare and ungrateful without them; they have saved hours of boredom and provided hours of comfort and warmth to lost and delayed travellers'.

Opposite below: a location facing a major traffic junction and an Underground station makes the Belle Vue, 1 South Side, Clapham Common, Lambeth, a focus for animated encounters and a stance for the observers of the human scene whom the Victorians called 'loafers'.

The formidable public houses built on London's
corner sites in the second half of the nineteenth
century could hardly be mistaken for any other
sort of building. Above: the Kensington Arms,
Warwick Road, Kensington, photographed in the
late 1890s. Huge signboards, handsomely inscribed, soar two storeys high to the balustrade
and march along the skyline, proclaiming the
availability of Watney & Company's 'Genuine
Porter, Celebrated Old & Mild Pimlico Ales &
Imperial Stout'. Much the same message is trans-
mitted at the Archway Tavern, Highgate,
opposite. So comprehensive an advertisement of
the brewer's range of products usually meant, by
this point of time, that he owned the premises.
Until the 1870s, most public houses in the London
area were held on lease by publicans. It was
customary to pay the premium due to the ground
landlord on the grant of the lease by borrowing
the money from a brewer, in return for contracting
to buy that brewer's beer. If the publican fell out

with the brewer, he could pay off the loan by
transferring his custom to another brewer. This
cosy arrangement was killed by the events set in
train by an Act of 1869 which restored jurisdiction
over beerhouses to the magistrates, thus bringing
to an end the experiment in 'free trade in ale and
ale-houses' that Parliament had inaugurated
thirty-nine years earlier. The magistrates then set
themselves the congenial task of reducing the
total numbers of public houses by refusing to
renew the annual licences of those they considered
'redundant'. This policy inevitably put a premium
on the market value of public houses at the upper
end of the commercial scale, and rendered potential
victims almost worthless. In the ensuing scramble
to secure the trade of a dwindling number of retail
outlets, brewers competed to buy up freeholds,
especially after 1880, when loans free of a brewer's
tie became available from other sources. So the
'loan tie' or 'mortgage tie' was placed by a
landlord and tenant relationship.

The Archway Tavern was rebuilt in 1886 in a key position at the foot of Highgate Hill on the Great North Road. It had been the northern terminus since 1872 of the tramway lines to Euston, King's Cross and Moorgate. Some rewarding sites have been occupied by a public house, in successive reincarnations, for centuries. 'In the south suburbs, at the Elephant, is best to lodge', Antonio advised Sebastian in *Twelfth Night*; Shakespeare, as usual, had London in mind. The Elephant and Castle, Southwark; the Angel, Islington, and the Swiss Cottage, Hampstead, all located at major crossings of main roads into London, were terminals or halts on omnibus or tramway routes before their names were applied to Underground stations.

Much importance was attached to the exploitation of prominent sites. By the exercise of ingenuity, a public house could be designed to dominate the scene and to draw in pedestrians susceptible to impulse-buying. Above: the florid, gin-palace revival style of the Alfred's Head, 140 Newington Causeway, Southwark, was calculated to dazzle: literally so, with the help of ornate gas lanterns, taller than the men below, which take the place of classical urns on the balustrade. The photograph was taken in 1904. By contrast, the City of Salisbury, Tooley Street, Bermondsey,

opposite, turns the corner with elephantine grace. Built about 1888, it looks like a citadel of respectability in the heart of dockland. The machicolated parapet stirs faint memories of the Round Tower at Windsor Castle, and this may possibly have been the architect's intention. He must have had an interest in history. The chequer-board motif under the ground-storey windows is one of the oldest of tavern signs, used in that sense at Pompeii and in Hogarth's 'Beer Street', but seldom applied to new buildings in late Victorian times.

A large reduction in the number of outlets was recommended by a Royal Commission on the Liquor Licensing Laws, reporting in 1899. To achieve this end without patent injustice, the Licensing Act, 1904, set up a compensation fund from levies made on all licence-holders. The Birmingham justices, with the co-operation of the brewers, closed 648 licences between 1897 and 1904, and 391 thereafter. 'Fewer and better' was the watchword of this programme of planned distribution of licensed premises, achieved by Birmingham long before any other city. 'The fewer the better' was the interpretation preferred by a number of licensing benches. Below: the Bakers Arms, Crescent Street, Euston Square, London, and, opposite, the Star in the East, Hastings, are examples of thousands of humble, back-street public houses that were blotted out of existence. These two were 'compensated' in 1912 and 1913 respectively. They demonstrate, incidentally, how the signwriter's craft, used by Victorian brewers to superb effect, could transform the appearance of humdrum buildings by beautifully lettered advertisements.

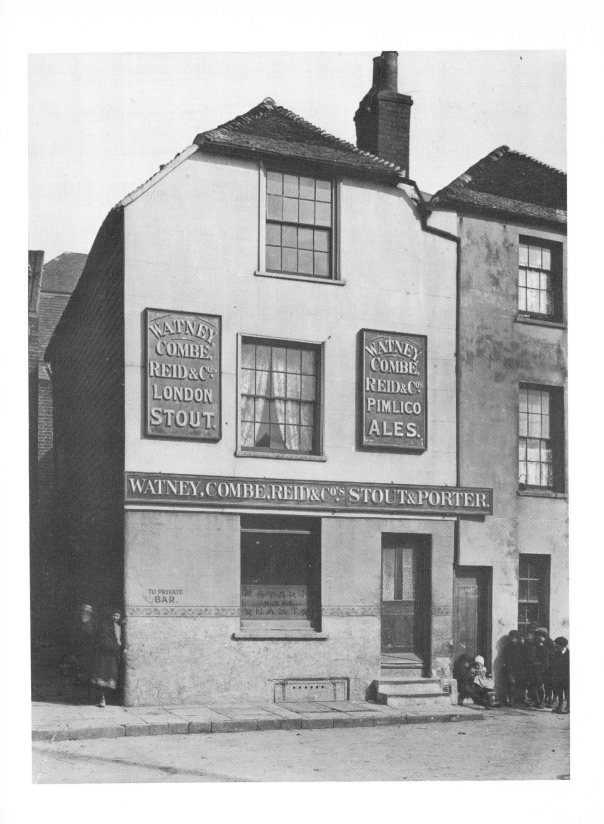

DUBLINERS

It is still impossible to visit one of the older Dublin pubs and imagine for a moment that you are at the Green Man or the George and Dragon, somewhere in England. The Dublin pub reflects a different social pattern and a different method of trading. The business is owned by the publican, not by a company. It is usually his name which is blazoned along the fascia, flanked by such words as 'Whiskey Bonder' and 'Wine and Spirit Merchant'. Neither term need be interpreted to mean exactly what it says. The first indicates that the publican is in the habit of buying whiskey in cask from the distiller, lodging it in a bonded warehouse and paying the excise duty when he withdraws it from bond for bottling and sale.

There are still a very few publicans in Dublin who do this. The practice is now discouraged by the Irish distillers, just as it was by the Scotch distillers in 1915; they much prefer to sell proprietary brands in bottle, and one imagines that publicans would find the modern method of buying more economical than carrying stocks of whiskey in wood. Inside the premises, there are few concessions to cosiness and not much to distract the mind from the business at hand: drinking creamy-headed pints of Guinness, or 'a ball of malt', meaning a large measure, or 'glass', of Irish whiskey. (A 'glass' is one-tenth of a bottle, as opposed to 'a half one', half a glass or one-twentieth of a bottle, the more usual measure.)

This single-minded concentration of function impregnates the atmosphere, even when the bar is deserted.

Opposite: Lynch's, Aungier Street. Note the rich, well-smoked patina of the matchboarded ceiling. The 'masculine brown harmonies' that Lewis Mumford noted in English bars may also be found in Ireland, though here too public houses of genuine Victorian character continue to disappear. Above: Another room at Lynch's. The aedicular partition serves as a screen and as a display case for wines and spirits.

Below: A 'snug' at Lynch's. This ultimate in privacy for cronies, an inner room reserved for favoured regular customers, is vanishing from the North of England, following its counterparts in the Midlands (the 'office bar') and in the South (the 'bar parlour'). In Ireland it survives. It is the occasional retreat of serious drinkers during 'Holy Hour', between 2.30 and 3.30 pm, when licensed houses in the cities of Dublin, Cork, Limerick and Waterford are required to close. This measure was enacted shortly after Irish independence, with the double object of encouraging bar-flies to find something else to do, and of allowing the 'curates', or publican's assistants, to take time off for lunch. The Irish Republic retains the Victorian system of 'closing hours', unlike Great Britain, where the Licensing Act, 1921, substituted 'permitted hours' of opening: nine in the Metropolis and eight elsewhere, on weekdays, with a break of not less than two hours in the afternoon. Opposite: Mullett's, Amiens Street. The off-sales department is sometimes combined with a small bar for white-collar customers. Off-sales customers are supplied through a hatch, left, without needing to enter the bar. The tier of drawers survives from the days when even town pubs sold groceries. Generally known as 'tea drawers', they might have held any kind of dry goods, such as sugar or spices. Their presence may be taken as a field identification character of an

unspoiled period pub. On top, between the two
40-oz bottles of John Jameson, mock-Staffordshire
figures of a hurler and a Gaelic footballer stand on
a plinth inscribed with a double pun: 'On all
grounds—Players please'. Centre, assorted objects
in dynamic repose, ready for emergency opera-
tions in the cellar: pulleys for raising the trap-door,
inspection lamp leads, a bicycle lamp, a packet of
candles, and hydrometer tables used in reducing
the strength of bulk spirits. This tiny space
is also used as the office, holding a roll-top
desk, a telephone, accounts on a spike, memor-
andum pads and a schedule of Dublin postal
charges.

CONTRASTS

Bedford Park, Ealing, begun in 1876, was the earliest of planned garden suburbs. It was developed by Jonathan T. Carr for people of moderate means and artistic tastes: *une veritable utopie*, according to Ernest Renan. Norman Shaw, the architect who laid out Bedford Park, tried to keep some of the atmosphere of rural Middlesex. He himself designed the focal group: the church, the 'Stores' and the 'Hostelry'. The Tabard, Bath Road, Chiswick, opposite, completed in 1880, reflects Shaw's study of domestic building in Sussex.

He had its public bar lined with tiles by William de Morgan and its upper room with cedar panelling from a City church. Early residents, many of whom shared William Morris's hatred of the contemporary urban scene, may have recognised the Tabard as a minor landmark in the history of taste. In building any sort of public house, the planners of Bedford Park were far ahead of their time. No public house was permitted, let alone expressly provided, in later 'garden cities' or 'garden suburbs': at Port Sunlight (begun c. 1888), Bournville (c. 1895), Letchworth (c. 1903), Hampstead (c. 1907), or at Welwyn in the 1920s.

One of the most powerful and original influences on domestic architecture of the early twentieth century was that of C. F. A. Voysey. He designed the Wentworth Arms, Elmesthorpe, Leicestershire, below, built in 1895: characteristic, with its high-pitched roof, wide eaves, tall chimneys, and bands of small-paned, small-sized windows, of his theory of building. The main purpose of these features is to retain domestic warmth and to keep the weather out. Voysey's houses are designed 'from within outwards', as he himself put it, so that their external appearance is shaped by 'practical requirements of accommodation, plan, aspect and prospect'.

The window's of the Wentworth Arms are proportioned to give breadth and lightness, inside and outside, to a very small building. Those in the main bar, above, are extended outwards to create a sense of spaciousness and to provide semi-isolated meeting places, such as that in the photograph. Voysey designed the window-seats and the plate-rack illustrated here, with the tiled fire-places and door-hinges and probably the original furniture, carpets, wall-papers and fittings. 'With all the objects of daily use', he wrote, 'if we train ourselves to look for signs of moral quality, we shall do much to encourage true culture and bring spiritual joy out of material mire'. There speaks the son of the Reverend Charles Voysey who was thrown out of the C. of E. for denying the doctine of hell-fire, and went on to found his own Theistic Church.

The Vines, Lime Street, Liverpool, built twelve years after the Wentworth Arms, is its converse in almost every respect. Very large, demanding attention with its billowing gables and giant, upthrusting turret, it is the sort of thing that Voysey derided as 'shirt-front architecture'. The interior, opposite, with its combination of engraved glass and carved mahogany, ornate plasterwork and stained glass, continues a tradition of late Victorian craftsmanship into its Edwardian afterglow. The richness of these interiors reflects Liverpool's self-confidence and pride at the height of its commercial prosperity.

'Pont Street Dutch' was Osbert Lancaster's nickname for the Chelsea and Kensington manifestations of the 'Queen Anne' manner used by Norman Shaw at Bedford Park. Gothic, associated with churches, chapels, institutions and moral uplift, was intrinsically unsuited to public house architecture; but very free variants of the post-Gothic fashion, applied to convey liveliness without loss of respectability, proved an acceptable building formula for the licensed trade in the 1890s. The plastic qualities of the style are well expressed in the 'Dutch' gables, turrets and bow-windows of the Philharmonic, Hope Street, Liverpool, below, built in 1898-1900. The architect was Walter Thomas, assisted by specialists in the sumptuous decoration of the interior. This is still remarkably Ninetyish in atmosphere, with a flavour of Art Nouveau: plaster caryatids, a curving bar counter faced with crimson and gold mosaic, repoussé copper panels,

and heavily moulded plasterwork. Light filters through screens and windows of stained glass, patterned with coats of arms, celebrating contemporary heroes, Roberts and Baden-Powell, or dedicated, in the room facing the Philharmonic Hall, to St Cecilia and to Longfellow's proposition that 'Music is the universal language of mankind'.

Above: the Great Northern Railway Tavern, High Street, Hornsey. Its name commemorates the most momentous event in the history of the parish—the arrival of the railway in 1850. Passengers waiting for the 8.45 up train at Hornsey Station in April 1866 watched a hare being coursed over the fields, and knew that they might never see that sight again, as first the leafy lanes, then the fields between, were filled to saturation by rows of bricky dwellings. Hornsey's rural character must have been almost obliterated by 1897, when the present Great Northern Railway Tavern, a thoroughly urban building, replaced its rustic predecessor. The eye-catcher in this formal composition is the gable. Its purpose is to frame the name of the house, blazoned out in letters made from small pieces of brick joined together and applied to the surface.

Anyone who dreams that he dwells in marble halls should have a pleasant time indulging his fantasy at the Crown, Aberdeen Place, Maida Vale. It dates from about 1892. The saloon bar, above, is sumptuously fitted out, with marble lining the walls, the canopy of the baronial fireplace and the counter, with elaborate woodwork and a strongly-patterned, coffered ceiling. The high-backed chairs, part of the original furnishings, went out of service shortly after this photograph was taken in 1967. The door on the right opens into a cavernous billiard room, commonly provided in the larger public houses of the Nineties, and here, uncommonly, still used as such. The keeping of billiard tables in public houses, forbidden by an eighteenth-century statute, was re-authorised by the Gaming Act, 1845, under which the justices may grant annual licences to 'fit and proper persons'. 'During the past fifty

years', Major-General A. W. Drayson confidently asserted in 1890, 'the game of Billiards has advanced from the disreputable to the highly respectable, and now deservedly occupies the position of a first-class indoor game'—a statement to be weighed against the opinion of Herbert Spencer's friend that to play billiards well was a sign of an ill-spent youth. Parliament and the judiciary have devoted much attention to determining what are 'lawful' and 'unlawful' games on licensed premises. In 1852 the judges decided (in Reg. v Ashton) that playing dominoes *for recreation only* could lawfully be 'carried on' in public houses. The principle of that judgement is enshrined in the Gaming Act, 1968, which singles out dominoes and cribbage as games that may be played on licensed premises without specific authorisation by the licensing justices, who may however impose restrictions to prevent play 'for high stakes', or 'in such circumstances as to constitute an inducement to persons to resort to the premises primarily for the purpose of taking part in any such gaming'.

Below: the Central, Ranelagh Street, Liverpool, located in the centre of the city, has a more intimate scale and plan than the Crown. The date incised on the façade is 1887. The walls of the front bar have a dado of green tiles decorated with an enigmatic, flowing pattern in the Art Nouveau manner. Above it, leading the eye upwards to an ornate, many-coloured dome, arcaded panels of engraved glass isolate the customers from the din and turmoil of the street, enveloping them in filtered light.

Two bars at the back of the building, reached by a tiled corridor from a separate entrance, afford an even greater degree of quiet and privacy: the smoke room, lined with glittering, brilliant-cut mirror glass, and the 'news room'. The latter is a North of England variant of the tap-room. Its name is derived from the long-disused practice of providing newspapers free, or hiring them out for a penny.

105

The exteriors of Victorian public houses were designed to bring the customers in, and the interiors to encourage them to remain and to come back another time. Just how the theory was put into practice varied from one generation to the next and depended always upon the character of the neighbourhood. Below: the King's Head, Upper Tooting Road, Wandsworth, dates from 1896, when Tooting, in Murray's words, was 'a region of villas and nursery-grounds without any special interest for tourists'. The King's Head was built to attract very short-range travellers. It is not a design that would have been accepted for exhibition by the Royal Academy; but then Mr John Piper, who has written better than anybody else about the qualities of public house architecture, told us long ago that 'the characteristic of the best and most successful public houses of any date . . . is not good taste, but a rich substitute for it. What is demanded—and more urgently than in any other type of building—is popular architecture'. If, as Mr Piper suggests, 'recognisable character' should be the criterion, the King's Head has certainly got something. Its

ripe, beery, music-hall jollity finds no echo in another building of the same period: the Gorse Hill Hotel, Chester Road, Stretford, Manchester, above. Dignity, reticence, and solid bourgeois worth may have been the qualities that the builders thought appropriate for a public house in the town centre. Its name, and Gorse Hill Park itself, recall the lost landscape devoured by the advancing city. Murray's comment on Stretford in 1870, 'the village is pretty and rural', may still have held good in the 1880s, when a notable pair of cricketers used to open for Lancashire at Old Trafford, 'O my Hornby and my Barlow long ago!' After 1896, when the Manchester Ship Canal had cut the place in two, and Trafford Park had been turned into England's first industrial trading estate, Stretford settled into its role of engineering town and middle-class dormitory, until that identity too was almost submerged in Manchester's.

107

Above: the Queen's, Broadway Parade, Crouch End, with its radiant windows of stained glass in Art Nouveau patterns, dates from about 1901, the year when Queen Victoria died. At the end of her reign, a substantial body of her subjects believed that public houses were a social nuisance, that the fewer there were the better, and that no public houses would be best of all. Hardly anyone believes that now. Drunkenness is no longer a major social problem, largely because the generation represented by the three men in this photograph, taken seventy years later, is incomparably better fed, better housed, better educated, enjoys better conditions at work and many more opportunities for recreation, than its Victorian forbears. A silent revolution in the habits of ordinary people, accomplished without much repressive legislation, has vindicated Archbishop Magee's opinion in 1872 that 'it would be better that England should be free than that England should be compulsorily sober . . . because with freedom we might in the end attain sobriety; but in the other alternative we should eventually lose both freedom and sobriety'. Today, with other well-organised commercial interests competing to entertain the masses, the public house is no longer so dominant an influence in working-class life; but it has gained by becoming more acceptable to the whole nation in, thank God, a less class-ridden society. In George Orwell's words, it is one of the basic institutions of English life.

BIBLIOGRAPHY

Anon. 'The Business of Pleasure', *All the Year Round*, 10, 10 October 1863

Anon. *London at Dinner* (1858, reprinted 1969)

Baedeker, Karl. *London: Handbuch für Reisende* (1866); *London and its Environs* (1879, 1889, 1900)

Barker, T. C. and Robbins, Michael. *A History of London Transport*, 1 (1963)

Barnard, Alfred. *The Noted Breweries of Great Britain and Ireland* (1889-91)

Betjeman, John. 'C. F. Annesley Voysey: the Architect of Individualism', *Architectural Review*, 70 (1931)

Booth, Charles. *Life and Labour of the Poor in London* (1892-1902)

Brett, C. E. B. *Buildings of Belfast* (1967)

Callingham, J. *Sign writing and glass embossing* (1871)

Cunningham, Peter. *A Handbook to London* (1849)

Dickens, Charles. *Sketches by Boz* (1836); *American Notes* (1842); *Collected Papers* (1903)

Drayson, Maj Gen A. W. (ed). *Handbook of Games* (1890)

Esquiros, Alphonse. *L'Angleterre et la vie anglaise*, 1ère série (1861)

Gorham, Maurice. *Back to the Local* (1949)

Gorham, Maurice and Dunnett, H. McG. *Inside the Pub* (1950)

Grossmith, George and Weedon. *The Diary of a Nobody* (1892)

Guide-Chaix: Nouveau Guide à Londres pour l'Exposition de 1851 (1851)

Harrison, Brian. *Drink and the Victorians: the Temperance Question in England, 1815-72* (1971)

Harrison, Brian. 'The Power of Drink', *The Listener*, 13 February 1969

Hitchcock, Henry-Russell. *Early Victorian Architecture* (1954)

Hughes, J. Quentin. *Liverpool* (1969)

Knight, Charles (publisher). *London* (1841-43)

Larwood, Jacob. *History of Signboards* (1866)

The London Post Office Directory (1842-1903)

Longmate, Norman. *The Waterdrinkers: a History of Temperance* (1968)

Loudon, John Claudius. *Cyclopaedia of Cottage, Farm and Villa Architecture*, revised by Mrs Loudon (1857)

Margetson, Stella. 'The Rise of the Luxury Hotel', *Country Life*, 13 November 1969

Mathias, Peter. *The Brewing Industry in England 1700-1830* (1959)

Molyneux, F. *Burton-on-Trent* (1868)

Murray's Handbooks for Travellers: Ireland (1866); *Shropshire, Cheshire and Lancashire* (1870); *Kent* (1892) and *Surrey* (1897)

Palmer, Arnold. *Movable Feasts* (1957)

Papworth, Wyatt. *John B. Papworth, Architect to the King of Wurtemburg* (1879)

Paterson's Licensing Acts, 68th ed. (1970)

Pevsner, Nikolaus. *London* (1952)

Piper, John. *Buildings and Prospects* (1948)

Reader, W. J. *Life in Victorian England* (1964)

Richards, J. M. 'Pub at Peckham Rye', *Architects' Journal*, 30 May 1957

Ridley, J. G. *Lord Palmerston* (1970)

Robbins, Michael. *Middlesex* (1953)

Scott, Harold. *The Early Doors* (1946)

Scott, Harold. 'The Pub Music Hall', *Architectural Review*, 105 (1949)

Spiller, Brian. 'The Story of Beer', *Geographical Magazine*, 28, nos 2, 3 and 4 (1955)

Sugden, A. V. and Edmondson, J. L. *A History of English Wallpaper* (1925)

Symonds, R. W. and Whineray, B. B. *Victorian Furniture* (1962)

Timbs, J. C. *Club Life of London*, 2 (1868)

Victoria, Queen. *Letters*, 3rd series, 1891-95 (1931)

Voysey, C. F. A. '1874 and After', *Architectural Review*, 70 (1931)

Wakefield, Edward Gibbon. *England and America* (1833)

ACKNOWLEDGEMENTS

For permission to reproduce photographs, prints or engravings on the pages listed below, I wish to thank the following: Patrick Rossmore, frontispiece, 64, 66; London Borough of Hammersmith, Public Libraries, 7; Corporation of London, Guildhall Library, 8, 13-14, 32, 44-5, 48, 55 (above); Watney Mann Ltd, 18-19, 21, 28, 46, 89; Clive Piper, 27, 30, 34-5, 87 (below), 92-3; Bath Academy of Art, 20, 29, 58, 64, 70-1, 74-81, 100-2, 105, 108; Corporation of Norwich, Public Libraries, 22-3; Victoria & Albert Museum, Crown copyright, 24-5, 52-3; London Borough of Lambeth, Public Libraries, 26; London Borough of Greenwich, Public Libraries, 36, 40-1; E. P. Olney, 47; London Borough of Islington, Public Libraries, 33, 50; Ind Coope Ltd, 62-3, 86, 91, 98, 103; Air Ministry Photographic Reproductions Branch, 68-9; National Monuments Record, Crown copyright, 54, 67, 72-3, 82-3; Bernard Heine, 55 (below), 87 (above), 99, 106; London Borough of Camden, Public Libraries, 60; by courtesy of London Borough of Tower Hamlets Libraries Committee, 84; London Borough of Brent, Willesden Central Library, 85; Royal Borough of Kensington & Chelsea, Central Library, 88; London Borough of Southwark, Public Libraries, 90; Arthur Guinness Son & Co (Dublin) Ltd, 94-7; Greater London Council Photograph Library, 59, 104; and Whitbread & Co Ltd, 107.

I am especially grateful to Bath Academy of Art, School of Visual Communications, for allowing me to take part in a group project on Victorian public houses, and to use photographs taken by Peter Juerges, Mary Komocki, Susan Legouix, Lynn Lewis and Alice Mitchell under the supervision of Barbara Luthy; to Colonel W. M. Maffett and to Arthur Neal for reproduction photography; to Ben Davis, George Engle, Graham Hayter, Colette Redmond and Douglas Shepherd for help in obtaining photographs; to the librarians who have given help in tracking sources of illustration, and particularly to the staff of the London Library, and of the Guildhall Library, London, for unfailing courtesy and patience; to the Brewers' Society, Courage (Eastern) Ltd and the National Trade Development Association for information on particular buildings; to J. L. Lombard and to John Stace for technical advice; to Professor Peter Mathias for two quotations; and to Bernard Heine for creative criticism and encouragement. The responsibility for all errors of fact or of judgement is entirely mine.

INDEX

The names of public houses illustrated in this book are printed in capital letters. An asterisk after the heading means that the building is known to have been demolished, or substantially altered, since the photograph or drawing was taken.